VAGUS NE

ALL YOU NEED TO KNOW ABOUT THE VAGUS NERVE. HOW IT CAN INFLUENCE ANXIETY, DEPRESSION, AND MOOD IN GENERAL. LEARN HOW TO ACTIVATE AND STIMULATE IT.

Author: *Antony Wilson*

Copyright 2019 - All rights reserved.

The content contained within this book may not be reproduced, duplicated or transmitted without direct written permission from the author or the publisher.

Under no circumstances will any blame or legal responsibility be held against the publisher, or author, for any damages, reparation, or monetary loss due to the information contained within this book, either directly or indirectly.

Legal Notice:

This book is copyright protected. It is only for personal use. You cannot amend, distribute, sell, use, quote or paraphrase any part, or the content within this book, without the consent of the author or publisher.

Disclaimer Notice:

Please note the information contained within this document is for educational and entertainment purposes only. All effort has been executed to present accurate, up to date, reliable, complete information. No warranties of any kind are declared or implied. Readers acknowledge that the author is not engaging in the rendering of legal, financial, medical or professional advice. The content within this book has been derived from various sources. Please consult a licensed professional before attempting any techniques outlined in this book.

By reading this document, the reader agrees that under no circumstances is the author responsible for any losses, direct or indirect, that are incurred as a result of the use of the information contained within this document, including, but not limited to, errors, omissions, or inaccuracies.

INTRODUCTION 6

CHAPTER 1. WHAT IS THE VAGUS NERVE? 10

The Vagus Nerve 11
The Vagus Nerve Matters 14
Where is the Vagus Nerve Located? 17

CHAPTER 2. HOW THE VAGUS NERVE CONTROL IT ALL 18

CHAPTER 3. WHAT HAPPENS IF SOMETHING COULD GO WRONG IN VAGUS NERVE? 28

About Breathing Problem 28
About Heart Rate Problem.. 30
About Microbiome Problem... 34

CHAPTER 4. VAGUS NERVE ON CHRONIC STRESS, CHRONIC INFLAMMATION, AND DIGESTIVE PROBLEM 36

Chronic Fatigue and Your Vagus Nerve 37
Chronic Inflammation and the Vagus Nerve 38
Problems on Digestion 39

CHAPTER 5. DYSFUNCTIONAL SLEEP AND CIRCADIAN RHYTHM PROBLEM 41

CHAPTER 6. DEPRESSION AND THE VAGUS NERVE 47

Defining Depression... 47
Depression and the Vagus Nerve 49
Methods in Fighting off Depression 50
   Probiotics to Stimulate the Vagus Nerve............................... 50
   Socialization to Stimulate the Vagus Nerve........................... 52
   Meditation to Stimulate the Vagus Nerve 53

CHAPTER 7. VAGUS NERVE RELATION TO ANXIETY 56
What is Anxiety? 56
Signs of Anxiety 59
How to Deal with the Anxiety Vagus Nerve 61

CHAPTER 8. THE RELATION BETWEEN THE VAGUS NERVE AND PHOBIA & TRAUMA 64
The Vagus Nerve and the Phobias 64
The Vagus Nerve and Trauma 69

CHAPTER 9. THE VAGUS NERVE AND ANGER 74
Anger 74
When Anger Becomes a Problem 76
Anger and the Vagus Nerve 76

CHAPTER 10. HOW TO ACTIVATE THE VAGUS NERVE 78
Take Care of Your Digestive Tract 82
Shake it off 83
It's getting a Bit Chilly Here 83
Diaphragmatic Breathing 85
Humming 85

CHAPTER 11. METHODS TO ACTIVATE THE VAGUS NERVE 88
Yoga 88
Meditation 90
Foods 94
Physical Therapy 96
Breathing 97

CONCLUSION 99

Introduction

The body has an extremely self-healing power. Our bodies have natural self-defense mechanisms that function by identifying changes in our environment and eliciting an appropriate response to these potential dangers in our surroundings. The body is equipped to defend itself without cognitive input. Without these natural reflexes, we would not be able to get ourselves out of harm's way. Therefore, these natural defense mechanisms are crucial for survival. These innate responses are facilitated by a system in our bodies. And these are responsible for the sensation and regulation of the stimuli. This system is responsible for receiving information from the environment around us and generating the appropriate reaction to that information. This system is called the nervous system.

The vagus nerve is the body's primary parasympathetic nerve. It supplies parasympathetic fibers to all the body organs, including the major organs such as the heart and lungs. It is the critical pathway for the transmission of information between the brain and other body organs and tissues. The vagus nerve, as a result, enables the brain to monitor functions of various body organs and systems in the body.

By learning how to hack into the powers of the vagus nerve, you will significantly improve your health and facilitate a natural pathway that the body can use to heal and repair itself naturally. Good health stems from in-depth knowledge of how our body works and what we can do to ensure that essential elements such as the Vagus nerve are consistently stimulated and active.

The vagus nerve is so powerful that it connects and influences other nerves. It's not something that's taught in school or throughout life, but it's something incredibly important to the health and wellness of our bodies. It's a nerve in our brains that some of us don't even know about. But, the vagus nerve plays a significant role in both problems with the body, and also helps correct existing issues.

While the vagus nerve functions naturally, age and other stress factors can inhibit its activity leading to a decreased vagal tone. It means that we need to equip ourselves with the knowledge on how to stimulate and activate the vagus nerve to reap its self-healing benefits. An active Vagus nerve means that our bodies can achieve a state of equilibrium between the parasympathetic and sympathetic nervous systems. When either system is not balanced out by the actions of the other, we tend to develop physical and psychological disorders that impact our quality of life

This book will cover all you need to know about vagus nerve stimulation, what it is, why it matters, and why stimulating this nerve could account for solving many of the problems you may be currently experiencing.

The book begins with a very structured breakdown of what the vagus nerve is, what it affects, and the biology of this complex system. The deeper you can grasp the concept of the vagus nerve, the easier it will be for you to understand the symptoms you experience and how they're related to your vagal system.

Welcome to the first few pages of a journey toward healing based on knowledge and understanding of critical systems within our body. This journey will take us through the body's autonomic nervous system (ANS) —specifically the vagus nerves—and how this nervous system impacts your health.

This book will serve as your introduction to the nerve itself, as well as its functional capabilities and the processes it uses to achieve those capabilities. It will provide guided exercises for you to practice, stimulating your nervous system to increase your health and the overall balance of your body. In coming to understand the needs your body places on this nerve, you will be able to activate it to balance out your stress and anxiety—often taxing biological responses that can leave you drained and feeling like a shadow of yourself.

This title will cover the foundation of the vagus nerve and what it does for you day in and day out, but this guide will also seek to help you heal and overcome trauma and pain associated with the vagus nerve. To do so, you need to have an understanding of what the nerve does to gain perspective of how the exercises in this book can affect such a delicate system and do so safely for your benefit.

Remember that you don't have to go through this journey alone. Ask for medical advice from your doctor or physician before starting any intense treatment, and seek their advice in areas where you are unsure of the best approach. Hope exists for those who suffer from vagus nerve-related issues, and the answers to your health conditions might be lying within these words.

The body itself works off cues it receives from the multitude of chemical, electrical, and nervous impulses sent through it based on stimuli, fuel, and even alien invaders to our enclosed biological systems. Environmental cues also play a role, interpreted by our brains through our senses, and the parasympathetic system not only displays social cues for others to interpret but allows us to see and interpret those reactions in them.

Chapter 1. What Is The Vagus Nerve?

You need your nerves. That much is certain. When your nerves function well, your whole body becomes capable of becoming the well-oiled machine it needs to be. The vagus nerve, however, becomes a sort of commander of the majority of your organs. As a cranial nerve, your vagus nerve has a very special function—it is capable of taking stimulation from your body straight to the brain without it having to go through alternate pathways. If you were to imagine all of your nerves existing as a sort of transit system, complete with all sorts of stops along the way, your cranial nerves would be like the express routes. They get you from point A to B without having to go between other intermediaries. While other signals throughout your body will route back through your spinal cord, your vagus nerve is a direct line of travel from the body to the brain. We are going to be discussing the vagus nerve in-depth, learning how it works and what you can expect from it. When you understand how your vagus nerve works and why it matters, you can begin to identify the areas impacted in your life by it in some way. You would get shocked to see that, all along, you had a low vagal tone, implying that your vagus nerve is not firing properly. Your vagal tone is how we determine how functional that vagus nerve is. While it can be checked through directly connecting to the vagus nerve to identify just how much activity is occurring within it, there are other methods that you can use as well. In particular, you can discover the health of your vagus nerve through the variation in your heart rate during your inhales and exhales. When there is a more significant variation between the inhale and exhale, it is believed that the vagus nerve is more powerful—it is referred to as toned. When you see very little variability, however, you may have other secondary problems occurring as well, and that is when you want to start considering interventions to help support it.

The Vagus Nerve

The vagus nerve is a pair of cranial nerves that originate from the base of the brainstem. They travel down from the brainstem in several different branches that reach across much of the body. In particular, this nerve is named vagus from the same root word of a vagabond—it means wanderer. It was aptly named, the vagus nerve travels throughout the face, the neck, the torso, and the abdomen, innervating several different areas and influencing how they work.

In particular, the vagus nerve is sensorimotor. This means that, while most nerves are specialized one way or the other, the vagus nerve can communicate both to and from the brain. It allows for sensation and sensory data to be taken to the brain, which is where the afferent nature comes into play. However, it also sends commands from the brain to the rest of the body to control it, which is where it gets its efferent ability. It can not only make sense, but moves the body around you.

As a general rule, if you need to remember between afferent and efferent, try using this quick mnemonic: Afferent nerves arrive at the brain with their information while efferent nerves exit the brain with their information. Afferent nerves are your sensory nerves that would need to be able to send information straight to the brain to have it processed properly. Efferent nerves are your motor nerves that are responsible for moving your muscles and controlling your body, even if the muscles moved are the involuntary muscles of your organs that keep you alive.

This particular nerve, however, is important just since it is so wide-reaching, and due to the wide range of control, it has over the body. It is intricately involved in your emotional regulation, determining how you handle stress and how you interact with other people. It is responsible for ensuring that you are capable of functioning as a whole thanks to the intermediary that it plays between all of these important body parts and the brain.

In particular, you can see the vagus nerve serving as a sort of regulator of the autonomic nervous system. It allows for the fear responses that people have. That fear response is what the body needs to be ready and able to interact with the world. Think about it—if you had to consciously consider the pros and cons of running away from a tiger instead of fighting the tiger off, there is a good chance that you would spend so much time deliberating between the two that instead, you would wind up getting attacked long before you made a decision. Because of that, the vagus nerve takes control of you. It makes these sorts of snap-decisions for you, so you do not have to make them instead. It removes that delay of having to decide what you do so you can react instinctively consciously. You respond with that same primal part of your brain that will lead other animals to react to their surroundings. You will usually either fight, run away, or freeze up altogether. Still, it happens without you making the decision yourself to save you crucial time that will otherwise be better spent keeping you alive.

The Vagus Nerve Matters

The vagus nerve matters greatly in many different contexts, as well. We will be getting to the control of the autonomic nervous system later, but for now, let's look at the four main functions that the vagus nerve performs. Each of these functions is integral to keeping the body alive, as you will very quickly come to realize going over it all.

Firstly, the vagus nerve is sensory, as we have identified. It allows the body to register and recognize sensations so the brain can process it. In particular, your vagus nerve will allow you to recognize sensory information from the throat, in particular around the vocal cords. It allows for sensory information from the heart and lungs, regulating them as well. Finally, it reaches down into the abdomen to allow for sensory information from the digestive system to help regulate everything accordingly.

It also involves special sensory information transmission. These special sensory transmissions are those related to your senses. They are the senses of sight, smell, taste, hearing, and balance in particular. The vagus nerve relates specifically to the sense of taste. Though it is not the primary cranial nerve involved in the sensation of taste, it innervates the back of the tongue, which allows for some tasting to occur.

The vagus nerve is also involved in motor functions, in particular relating to the neck. It controls your ability to swallow and speak. However, it does more than this as well—it goes down into your abdomen and works with your ability to digest food. It can provide that feedback to the body to make sure that the digestive tract goes accordingly and to make sure that you feel hungry when you need to.

Finally, it is strongly involved in parasympathetic functioning, which allows it the complete control over the digestive tract, your breathing, and your heart rate. The more or less active than the parasympathetic response is, the more or less calm you will feel. We will be looking at this further. However, beyond just these four categories, it has many other effects on the body as well, including:

- Facilitating the communication between the gut and the brain: It is directly responsible for the transmission of information between the two.

- Facilitating relaxation: It is responsible for when your body begins to relax through its control over stress hormones.

- Decreasing inflammation: The vagus nerve is capable of sending out anti-inflammatory hormones to stop cytokines, which can otherwise wreak havoc on the body.

- Regulating heart rate and blood pressure: The vagus nerve can directly hinder the heart, slowing down the heart rate as a response to be highly stimulated. Sometimes, excessive stimulation of the vagus nerve can even lead to fainting.

- Managing the fear response: The vagus nerve determines how you will respond to stressors around you, directly influencing how you behave when you are faced with some sort of threat. It will decide whether or not you will fight, run away, or freeze up altogether.

Where is the Vagus Nerve Located?

The vagus nerve (also referred to as the 10th cranial nerve, CN X) is a very long nerve beginning in the brain tube and running across the neck and chest and abdomen. When both motor and sensory information are present, the heart contains innervation, large blood vessels, airways, kidneys, esophagus, stomach, intestines. Although there are two vagus nerves, the left and the right, doctors generally refer to them as a "vagus nerve." It plays a critical role in controlling the heart rate and maintaining a proper gastrointestinal tract. The vagus nerves also transmit sensory input back to the brain from the internal organs.

Chapter 2. How the Vagus Nerve Control It All

The vagus nerve is the conductor of a symphony orchestra for the human body. It controls the activity of so many different organs and cells in our body, but only when it functions optimally can it do so. The body's multiple organs and cells must be capable of detecting and communicating correctly. Dysfunctional signaling can result in a loss of equilibrium in the system, and ultimately a disorder and disease state.

Let's break down all of the various functions the human body orchestra conductor performs— the vagus nerve.

Sensing Skin of the Ear

The first branch of the vagus nerve is the auricular branch, which is directly involved in feeling the skin of the ear's auricle, tragus, and external auditory canal.

This branch's function is pure in sensation, allowing us to feel pressure, touch, temperature, and moisture on each ear's central section. This is clinically relevant and quite significant, as this is one of the major areas where the VN can be activated using therapies such as acupuncture.

Allowing Food to Be Swallowed

The second branch of the VN (the pharyngeal branch) regulates the activation of five pharynx muscles: The three constrictor muscles at the back of the throat and two other muscles that link the throat and the soft palate (the soft tissue at the back of the mouth's roof). This VN branch also regulates the active motor part of the gag reflex.

This is clinically important, as poor vagus nerve function will lead to coughing and a change in gag reflex function.

Managing Your Airway and Vocal Chords

Superior and frequent laryngeal nerves are the third and fourth branches of the VN. The muscles above the vocal cords are responsible for the superior laryngeal branch while the recurring laryngeal branch is responsible for the muscles below the cords.

The recurrent laryngeal branch carries motor information to the muscles below the vocal cords, allowing the vocal cord structures to form sounds by opening, closing and tensioning. It also has a sensory component that relays information of these structures from the esophagus, trachea, and internal mucous membranes. Dysfunction of these nerves during physical activity contributes to heaviness, speech loss and trouble breathing.

Controlling Breathing

The VN's pulmonary branch runs into the pulmonary plexus, connects to the sympathetic nervous system, and innervates both lungs' trachea and bronchi. The vagus component is a sensory nerve that relays information about lung expansion levels to the brain, as well as the levels of oxygen and carbon dioxide.

Controlling Heart Rate

The VN plays an important role in ensuring the heart rate stays within a comfortable range when the body is not under threat. Without the VN, our heart would not be working close to its optimum pace.

The vagus nerve is connected directly to the sinoatrial node, which sends electrical signals to the two atria (the thinner chambers at the top of the core). It is also connected directly to the atrioventricular node which manages the ventricles ' pumping rate and contraction pressure (the two thicker, lower chambers of the heart).

Maintaining Optimal Blood Pressure

The vagus nerve relays information from and to the kidneys to help it control the flow of water and urine from within the kidney glomeruli, the kidney's essential filtration unit while controlling the body's internal blood pressure. When the body is under stress, through the vagus and sympathetic nerves, signals from the blood vessels (in particular the carotid body) are relayed up the brainstem and back down to the kidneys. The kidneys then restrict their blood vessels and increase blood pressure by reducing the amount of water from the bloodstream being filtered out. When the body is calm, carotid body impulses instruct the kidneys to pump out more water and dilute the blood vessels to relieve blood pressure.

Controlling the Many Functions of the Liver

When the body is calm and at rest-digest, the activation of the vagus nerve decreases and the blood flow to the liver increases. During these times, priority is given to feeding, blood filtration, and other cellular flourishing functions.

The vagus nerve also controls the liver cells that produce bile and bile salts, as well as transporting bile into the gallbladder and small intestine. It has been shown that these cells, called cholangiocytes, are active when the vagus nerve is active, and increase bile flow to the gallbladder for storage.

Activating Gall Bladder Emptying

If the central nervous system suggests that fats are ingested, then the vagus nerve will quickly signal that bile will be required for the liver and gallbladder.

After receiving this signal, the gallbladder stimulates the smooth muscle cells in its lining and pumps the bile out into the small intestine through the bile duct to aid in the absorption of food. The gallbladder will remain full without this vagus nerve signal, and will not drain out the requisite bile—a condition known as obstructive cholestasis.

Managing Hunger and Satiety

The vagus nerve mediates the following controls in terms of carbohydrate metabolism: When blood sugar levels gradually decrease, afferent vagal fibers in the liver, increase activity and signal to the brain that more carbohydrates are required by the liver cells. Nevertheless, this mechanism does not signal abrupt changes in blood sugar; these are detected immediately within the brain.

The vagus nerve provides yet another road to satiety sensations. After eating a meal, vagal afferent neurons transmit information to the brain about the number of fats, particularly triglycerides and linoleic acid that have made their way to the liver. This activates the function of the vagus nerve and sends a signal to the brain, which produces a feeling of satiety and a desire to stop eating.

Managing Blood Sugar and Insulin Levels

Our bodies shift their balance towards the sympathetic nervous system during times of stress and release more of the adrenal stress hormones, specifically cortisol. Cortisol's primary effect is to increase blood sugar by stimulating a process called gluconeogenesis, which is when new glucose is created from fat and protein stored in the hepatic system.

In short bursts, it is necessary to use the sympathetic nervous system to keep us alive and to allow us to survive. In this situation, when our bodies have to shift to survival mode when the stressor approaches us. We either have to combat the threat, or take the flight and escape as quickly as possible.

Managing the Release of Digestive Enzymes from the Pancreas

When we eat, our small intestine taste buds and sensory cells send signals to the brain that determine the specific macronutrients present in the meal. Is it protein, fat and starch in the meal? How much of the digestive tract has reached each, and how fast? Once the answers to these questions are determined, the vagus signal the pancreas to release specific digestive enzymes — proteases, lipases, and amylases — to assist in the breakdown of these macronutrients, allowing our cells to digest these nutrients and eventually use them properly.

Managing Gut Motor Function

It is an important role of the vagus to get food from the mouth to the opposite end of the digestive tract. We chew that food down in our mouth after taking a bite of food until it is physically able to be swallowed and transported through the rest of the digestive tract.

Managing the Activity of the Immune System

The immune system can run amok without its brakes and start attacking human cells, which can lead to autoimmunity, or even stop attacking tumor cells which can lead to cancer. The immune system can be quite risky, without a system to keep it in check.

Overview of the Immune System

The Body's defensive system is the immune system. It protects you from invaders and unwanted toxins that can lead to unfavorable health conditions, and often does so. This system includes white blood cells, that send out sensors to search for body invaders. We roam through the bloodstream in an optimum working environment, identifying proteins and pathogens that have invaded the body and sending signals to other immune cells whose role is to remove such invaders which should not be present.

Managing Inflammation in the Gut

Through this mechanism, the vagus nerve uses the neurotransmitter acetylcholine (ACh) to send signals to the cells of the immune system throughout the body but especially strong signals in the gut. These impulses are designed to soothe immune response and reduce inflammation.

Allowing Us to Create Memories

The vagus nerve is heavily involved in relaying microbial information from the intestinal bacteria to the brain. This communication chain could be responsible for activating the production of a protein called neurotrophic factor (BDNF) derived from the brain. BDNF activation leads to increased neuronal connectivity, and most importantly, to memory production in the brain.

That means it can be difficult to form new memories and create new neuronal connections without gut bacteria and a healthy functioning vagus nerve. To an even greater degree, this means that if you have an optimally functioning vagus nerve, you are likely to be able to form larger memories and associations with the world around you and those that matter to you.

We are creating defenses during our fetal development to shield us from external threats. One such barrier is the gut-blood barrier which protects us from bacteria (both good and bad) that may want to invade. It is made from the same cells that create our barrier to the blood-brain. This ensures that any infection that happens in the stomach and breaks down the intestinal barrier also can break down the blood-brain barrier.

Ever walked into a room, and forgot why you went into that room? Have you ever tried to say something quite simple, but couldn't find the right words to say? These problems are commonly referred to as brain fog, and are caused by higher than optimal levels of inflammation in the brain. Brain fog happens when the blood-brain barrier has partially broken down, and toxic impulses may enter the brain tissue, thereby reducing neuronal activity.

Brain fog shows the presence of inflammation in the brain caused by a blood-brain barrier that is less than optimal, and therefore poorly functioning gut lining or leaky intestines.

Chapter 3. What Happens If Something Could Go Wrong In Vagus Nerve?

About Breathing Problem

Most health problems associated with the Vagus nerve usually have dysfunctional breathing as one of their symptoms. This is because breathing is one of the most obvious functions associated with the Vagus nerve, making it one of the first insight into the condition of the Vagus nerve.

Breathing is the first thing we learn to do at birth. Most of our organs are already working in the womb, but the mother is breathing on our behalf when we are in the womb. The moment we come into the world, we must immediately start breathing. We wouldn't survive our first few seconds without breathing.

We have help, the midwife or doctor may clear the airway to allow air into the lungs. The main task falls to the central nervous system and the diaphragm. The diaphragm also needs help from the lungs, which are signaled to open or close by the Vagus nerve.

Our body learns to breathe properly as a baby through the diaphragm. We are using the major muscles to breathe instead of the accessory muscles.

As we grow up, the body may forget how to breathe through the diaphragm. This may be due to stress and other social factors. Proper breathing requires the belly to move, protruding in and out, and this clashes with some cultural values.

Some aspects of psychology believe that we copy other people's mannerisms and try to fit into society's idea of who we should be because we started in a position of inferiority. We are at the mercy of our parents, guardians and other adults when we are out in this world. We worship them, and we want to be like them. That is how we grow and learn. We learn to work by mimicking older people; we learn to speak by trying to remake the sounds that come out of their mouth. This process applies to several aspects of our life as we grow up. Even as adults, we still mimic others.

Like is said earlier, breathing through the diaphragm moves the abdomen a lot. This makes the person appear to have a big belly and look fat. Sure, a mildly protruding stomach doesn't technically make you fat, but our society has its standard of beauty. That standard prioritizes a thin and flat stomach.

In trying to fit into society's image of beauty, why try to hide the belly, and this affects breathing. This later becomes second nature to us that the body becomes used to it. It begins to breathe improperly.

The Repetitive hiding of the stomach may work, and it will seem like we are training the stomach muscles to maintain shape, but we are training the nerves that signal the muscles.

The increase of blood flow to the muscles allows it to grow. Since we trained the nerves to breathe improperly, we can also reteach it to breathe properly.

A nerve and muscle have to function often, or it will become slow and dysfunctional.

For superficial reasons, we have trained the body to breathe inefficiently and improperly from our teenage years, and this has become second nature, ingrained into our fibers. It affects the nerves that have not been appropriately utilized for so long. The phrenic nerves are not being properly utilized, the nerve that signals the lungs; the Vagus nerve is also not used properly.

About Heart Rate Problem

The sympathetic nerves and the Vagus nerve will dictate a change in the heart rate. The sympathetic nerves will try to increase the heart rate, but the Vagus nerves will try to keep it as slow as it can. A considerably low heart rate, especially under stress implies that the Vagus nerve is strong and functioning optimally. A strong Vagus nerve can also increase lifespan. Some research shows that a low heart rate can result in longer life. A well-functioning Vagus nerve keeps the heart rate low, which means that it can expand your lifespan.

A dysfunctional heart rate is due to the inability of the Vagus nerve to reduce it after the body encounters stress.

It takes the heart a few minutes to return to its resting value. This return to resting heart rate from a high heart rate after the stressors have activated the sympathetic muscles is called recovery. The amount of time it takes the body to recover depends on the Vagus nerve. A strong Vagus nerve allows you to calm your nerves and slow down your heart rate quickly. The opposite happens with a dysfunctional heart rate.

There is also the problem of the Vagus nerve over-functioning and the sympathetic nerves under-functioning. The job is split into two to maintain balance. The job of the parasympathetic nerves is to slow down the heart rate, while that of the sympathetic nerve is to quicken the heart rate. If the parasympathetic nerves are functioning more than the parasympathetic nerves, the heart rate will be too low due to an imbalance in the nervous system, and it can result in fainting, which is a temporary loss of consciousness. The medical term for fainting is called syncope. Fainting may not be directly life-threatening, but it is inconvenient at best. It can affect the ability to function properly. It can also be embarrassing if it happens at inconvenient times in public gatherings.

The person doesn't have to be sick or have an existing health condition. Syncope can occur in an otherwise healthy individual. Again, it doesn't have any long-term effect, neither is it life-threatening, but it can have a devastating effect on the mood and self-confidence.

Many people believe that a sudden physical head tilt can cause this imbalance. This includes motions like standing or sitting too fast after lying down for a long period of time—the sudden shift in posture results in the direction of blood flow and blood pooling location. The change is too sudden for the muscles of the heart too easily adjusting to. In our theoretical scenario, the blood pool location moves to the abdominal region from the chest area. This results in a change in blood pressure, reducing it significantly and thus triggering the episode. It is the job of the autonomic nerves to maintain blood pressure, and they have failed in the task. They try to regain control, and the person starts regaining consciousness when they do. The episode leaves the body drained, fatigued and nauseous.

Still, it doesn't talk about why the autonomous nervous system wasn't able to perform its duty properly during the change in posture. It was unable to regulate the blood vessels and the muscles of the heart properly enough to accommodate the action above. This reduction in the ability of the autonomic nervous system to regulate the nerves is called dysautonomia. Dysautonomia may be a hereditary disease. It can also be due to other non-hereditary diseases such as Ehlers-Danlos syndrome and Charcot-Marie-Tooth disease. It may also be a physical manifestation of other issues related to the digestive and autoimmune system such as Chiari malfunctions, physical trauma, surgery or pregnancy.

It may be due to the lack of some nutrients required by the components of the nervous system or due to the increasing level of toxins in the body. Conditions like these are due to the inability of the nerves to react quickly.

Dysfunctional breathing can also directly affect the nerves of the autonomous system and the organs that are innervated by them. Examples of these diseases are chronic neuroinflammation, ulcerative colitis, sarcoidosis, Sjogren's syndrome, Crohn's disease, Parkinson's disease and amyloidosis.

The severity of vasovagal syncope is different for people dealing with it. The condition may be mild or severe. You need to understand that vasovagal syncope is not a disease in itself. It is instead a symptom of another problem. A person experiencing fainting spells should visit the doctor. Neurological tests such as the MRI scan will probably be required. You may find out the problem, but sometimes vasovagal syncope is just a consequence of an improperly functioning autonomous nervous system, to be more specific, an overactive Vagus nerve and an underactive sympathetic nerve.

When the body doesn't seem to be able to regulate the blood pressure and heart rate accurately, this is usually the problem.

About Microbiome Problem

In the gastrointestinal tract, afferent vagus nerves control nourishment consumption. In any case, in stoutness, GI vagal reactions to improvements are altered, prompting a move away from satiety toward the expanded nourishment intake. 10 Vagal pathways that aren't working appropriately are engaged with the advancement of obesity and the failure to get in shape picked up.

Many investigations have indicated that the gut microbiota is associated with weight upkeep. The gut microbiota aids the generation of short-chain unsaturated fats (SCFAs), which thus brings about the creation of substances that would then be able to follow up on afferent vagus nerves to expand satiety. In particular, the SCFA butyrate can straightforwardly actuate vagal afferent nerves in the little intestine.

Gut hormones actuate vagal afferent neurons, the essential neural pathway by which data about ingested supplements arrives at the focal sensory system (CNS) to assume a job in both GI capacity and satiety. Vagal afferent neurons can likewise get impervious to the hormone leptin, which controls hunger. Moreover, in a rat model, a high-fat eating routine delivered changes in the gut microbiota, and this lopsidedness brought about gut irritation and "flawed gut." Through poisons getting away into the circulatory system, this prompted changes in the capacity of vagal neurons.

Another favorable position of the vagus nerve is that it can check the aggravation that happens as an individual puts on weight. The vagus nerve additionally can diminish insulin opposition. Specialists encouraged rodents either a high-fat eating regimen or a high-fat eating routine together with vagus nerve stimulation. The rodents presented to just a high-fat eating regimen built up various harming impacts in the cerebrum, including insulin obstruction, oxidative pressure, irritation, and the cell demise known as apoptosis, which all lead to intellectual decay.

In any case, the group encouraged a high-fat eating regimen together with vagus nerve incitement had an improvement infringes and cerebrum insulin affectability just as diminished mind mitochondrial brokenness and cell apoptosis. Vagus nerve incitement likewise improved intellectual capacity.

Then again, an excessively dynamic vagus nerve can assume a job in bulimia nervosa. Increments in the vagal afferent movement are connected to overeating and retching in this condition. 13 inhibiting vagal afferent action in subjects with extreme bulimia nervosa brings about a quick and articulated decrease in voraciously consuming food and spewing contrasted and controls just as diminished troublesome symptoms.

Chapter 4. Vagus Nerve on Chronic Stress, Chronic Inflammation, and Digestive Problem

Having too much stress isn't a good thing. Stress makes you depressed, anxious, and also angry, and it can affect your ability to make rational decisions, whether it's in daily life, or the long run.

It also affects your dopamine and serotonin levels, both of which are neurotransmitters that handle our mood. Your vagus nerve handles the variability of this whenever it can, and when you're relaxed, you have more dopamine, serotonin, and you'll feel better.

For many of us, stress is a healthy way to accomplish things, but with the way life can be, it can be almost too much in many cases, and affects vagal tone when we're stressed.

When you feel stressed, depressed, or anxious, your vagal tone changes, and frequently, you're more focused on negative emotions, and psychiatric conditions. Epilepsy also increases when your vagus nerve isn't properly stimulated.

You can measure this in different ways by looking at the EmWave2 waves which measure your heart rate variability, which shows your vagal tone too.

Higher vagal tone means everything is working better, and it can also help to stimulate your vagus nerve. You'll notice that when your vagus nerve is appropriately stimulated, you also respond to situations more positively, whether it be emotional, or physiological situations. Your brain and emotions are properly connected, and it can help offset the issues that mental illness causes to happen to you.

Your vagus nerve is the connection between your digestive system, brain, and other conditions. It also controls inflammation. But, your vagus nerve also handles mental health conditions, and there are many that your vagus nerve involves.

Chronic Fatigue and Your Vagus Nerve

Your vagus nerve controls how your body handles certain conditions. When it's overstimulated, your body is fighting with the sympathetic nervous system, which is always putting you on high alert. But, if you're always on high alert, it'll make you feel thirsty and fatigued all the time.

This isn't just temporary tiredness either, it's frequently a serious condition, where you feel fatigued no matter what you do, and no matter how hard you try, and it doesn't go away. This can be attributed partially to digestive and nerve health, but it does tie into the vagus nerve.

So yes, chronic fatigue is caused by your vagus nerve, and it can make things very hard on you. It's also due to the breathing you're doing, because many people who have trouble breathing frequently suffer from the improper vagal tone, and that's because people don't realize how impactful this can be on the body.

Chronic Inflammation and the Vagus Nerve

Since the vagus nerve is the primary source for the body and brain to communicate, allowing for feedback in both directions, it is primarily responsible for identifying when there is inflammation within the body. When it can find that inflammation, largely through detecting cytokines, the brain finds out about that inflammation. It can then make sure that the proper amount of anti-inflammatory hormones are released. This means that the inflammation is appropriately regulated—it is not too strong, nor is it to underwhelming.

This proper response leads to people with entirely normal, functioning inflammation levels when it is necessary. For example, when you are injured, or you get a minor infection, that inflammation is necessary. The body regulates itself. However, for some people, this inflammation response can be largely suppressed, leading to immunodeficiency. Those whose response is too strong; on the other hand, can find themselves struggling with highly responsive inflammatory responses that attack themselves.

Problems on Digestion

Dysfunction digestive systems are a common symptom of somatization. Consider how intense emotions can cause you to feel nauseous, give you a fluttering sensation in the stomach, or cause you to feel pain or discomfort in the abdomen. Many emotions, such as anger, sadness, excitement, or fear can trigger gastrointestinal issues. Because of the gut-brain connection, emotion, not only affects the gut, but gut health also affects your emotions. Digestive issues can have the most impact on health, causing:

- Muscle tenseness of the neck and shoulders
- Frequent headaches
- Difficulty sleeping and restlessness
- Tremors
- Weight issues
- Grinding of teeth
- Difficulty focusing
- Procrastination
- Withdrawal
- Excessive thinking or talking about stressful events

- Feelings of overwhelm
- Being indecisive
- Memory issues
- Mood swings
- Depression or frequently crying.

Chapter 5. Dysfunctional Sleep and Circadian Rhythm Problem

If every night you realize you keep on tossing and turning, you know how you are going to feel overnight – tired and out of sorts. Overlooking the advocated 7 to 9 hours of shut-eye every day does more than allowing you to feel dizzy and grumpy. The long-term consequences of sleep deprivation are not well documented yet.

It drains your psychological skills and places your bodily health in real peril. Science has linked inferior slumber together with all sorts of health conditions, from weight reduction to a diminished immune process.

Reasons for Sleep-deprivation

A short, sleep-deprivation is brought on by persistent insomnia or reduced grade of sleep. Getting greater than 7 hours of sleep on a normal basis can finally result in health impacts that affect your whole body. This might also result from an inherent sleep illness.

Your own body wants to sleep, as it requires food and air to work at its finest. While asleep, the body adjusts itself and interrupts its chemical balance. The human brain forges new relations and enables memory retention.

Without sufficient sleep, your brain and human body systems will not work normally. Additionally, it may radically decrease your well being.

An overview discovered that sleeping too little through the night increases the probability of premature death.

Sudden symptoms of sleep disorder incorporate:

- Excess sleepiness
- Yawning
- Irritability
- Daylight fatigue

Stimulants, such as caffeine, are not enough to reevaluate your system's deep dependence on sleeping. In reality, these may make sleep-deprivation worse, making it harder to get to sleep through the nighttime. This, then, might cause some cycle of night insomnia accompanied closely by day caffeine ingestion to compensate for the hours of shut-eye.

Behind the scenes, a chronic sleep disorder may interfere with the body's internal processes and also induce more than only the first symptoms and signs in the list.

Central Nervous System

In your entire body, this nervous system is where all information will pass through. Sleep is essential to keep it functioning correctly; however, chronic insomnia can interrupt the way the human body sends information via pathways shaped between nerve cells (neurons) in the brain, which enable you to remember new information, you've learned. Sleep stress leaves your brain drained; therefore, it cannot perform its duties.

You may also find it takes longer and is more difficult to focus on or learn new matters. The signs that your system ship might also be postponed, decreasing your nourishment and increasing your risk for injuries.

Sleep-deprivation also negatively impacts your mental skills and emotional condition. You will feel impatient or more likely to have mood swings. Additionally, it may undermine decision making creativity and processes.

If sleep-deprivation continues a long time, you might start having hallucinations -- hearing or seeing things which are not there. Too little sleep may also activate mania in those who are bipolar patients. Other emotional dangers include:

- Spontaneous behavior
- Stress
- Depression
- Paranoia
- Suicidal ideas

You may also wind up experiencing microsleep daily. Over these episodes, you will drift off for a couple of seconds or minutes without even realizing it.

Micro-sleep is outside of your control and will be particularly dangerous if you are driving. Besides, it can make you more vulnerable to injury as a result of trips and falls.

Circadian Rhythm

Your Circadian rhythm is your 24-hour clock which compels wakefulness and sleep. Disruptions in the biological clock have deep impacts on our bodies and our hormones. New research has identified genes related to your biological clock, also called clock enzymes, which may be the cornerstone for metabolic disorders such as diabetes, obesity, and insulin resistance. The clock has a more potent effect on appetite and metabolism. If someone's circadian rhythms are out of whack- by dysfunctional genes by not getting enough sleep, jetlag, or ingestion at odd times, the metabolic rate slows and hunger raises.

Traditionally, the mental performance was believed to become the principal controller of the circadian clock. We know that organs in your torso just like the liver, pancreas and the intestines all have their very own circadian rhythms. Each one produces enzymes, hormones, and other molecules at various times. The brain behaves more as a conductor of this symphony, coordinating the numerous organs. Kidney disorders happen when the brain isn't in sync with all the organs. Insulin resistance may be a classic instance of this, once the pancreas has gone out of connection with the liver and the brain, inducing insulin production to become excessive or too low.

Clock Genes

The discovery of clock genes has resulted in questions regarding how disruptions in circadian rhythm may bring about the metabolic disorder, also when adjusting dysfunctional rhythms might help treat ailments such as obesity and diabetes. As an instance, studies are underway to find out whether there's a perfect time daily to eat to help with fat reduction and blood glucose control.

Additionally, it is hard to undo the results of metabolic disorder once the brakes are put in place. Researchers have concentrated on your human body's internal clock to search for techniques to take care of metabolic disorders. The point is to learn in case your dysfunctional biological clock is your origin or the consequence of metabolic issues. It's the timeless "chicken-and-egg" scenario.

Evidence for the clock: Researchers realize that fat burning capacity and also the clock are all joined. Studies have reported variations in enzymes that control the biological clock in patients with obesity, hypertension and diabetes. In mice, mutations of this clock gene and other genes linked to the reproductive clock trigger insulin resistance and metabolic syndrome.

Chapter 6. Depression and the Vagus Nerve

When people think about mental health issues, the two that come to mind are typically anxiety and depression. Depression is the other most common mental health issue around the world, and many people suffer from it. It is estimated that somewhere around 15% of people will experience depression, either acute or chronic, at some point in their lives.

This disorder can be debilitating. It can be exhausting. It can be draining, and it can be destructive. It can lead to so many different problems, and that can be a major reason you would benefit from trying to solve the problem altogether. Instead of continuing to stress about the problem, you can defeat the problem.

Defining Depression

Depression itself is the feeling of negativity and hopelessness that people sometimes feel. It is a period in which there is a lack of interest in the world around you. You can feel like you do not want to engage with other people. You find that anything you used to be interested in is no longer compelling. You do not want to do anything at all frequently, and that can sometimes really just make the problem worse.

Depression can be debilitating for these people. Especially when severe, people who suffer from depression can find they do not have the energy for anything at all. They feel slow. They feel sleepy, even if they cannot sleep. They feel stuck. They feel unhappy. Even the activities that once brought them joy in life are no longer enjoyable, and they find that they cannot do anything about it. This is a major problem for people; it can hold them back.

The following symptoms most often characterize depression:

- You cannot regulate your mood up and regularly. Your mood is frequently or always down, and you cannot know how to bring it back up, no matter how hard you may try.

- Your appetite has fluctuated greatly, and you either eat more often now, or you do not want to eat at all.

- You struggle to sleep, or you sleep constantly. Either way, you always feel exhausted.

- Your mood is usually low, and you can find that you become very irritable sometimes.

- You are permanently fatigued; you cannot get yourself to move around because your body is just that exhausted that frequently.

- You struggle to focus on what matters to you. You cannot concentrate on the most important aspects of your life, and you feel like your mood is endlessly dull and foggy.

- You do not have an interest in anything at all, even when they used to bring you joy.

- You feel worthless, or like you do nothing but bring the world down.

- You may fixate on the idea of death or suicide.

Depression and the Vagus Nerve

Remember, when the body feels that something is entirely futile, it shuts itself off; it stops trying to continue moving forward. It finds there is no reason to continue, so it begins to shut down and slow down. When you go into a frozen state, this is what happens. Your body dulls your mind; your concentration struggles. You lose interest and responsiveness. You feel like you cannot move at all or like moving or doing anything at all would take far too much effort out of your life.

The vagus nerve, when it is overactive, can trigger what is known as a parasympathetic shutdown. This is the freeze response. It is a primitive response to fear, developed long before mammals developed their more modern, nuanced fight or flight system. It is believed that depression, at or at least, certain kinds of depression, may be linked to this.

Many types of depression can be found to be resistant to just about all treatment options. These people are known to have treatment-resistant depression, and yet, stimulating the vagus nerve has been shown to help these people begin to get back to their old normal.

It may also be the case that depression is related to inflammation, especially if inflammation is treated when you stimulate the vagus nerve. Nevertheless, regardless of whether the depression caused by the vagus nerve in the same way that anxiety was, one thing is known for sure—depression can be managed with the stimulation of the vagus nerve.

Within, we are going to consider three methods that you can use to begin fighting off depression. We are going to look at probiotics—these are relevant to the vagus nerve thanks to the prominent role that the vagus nerve plays in the digestive system and the digestive system's prominent role in the production of serotonin—which happens to be one of the ways that we can treat depression. We will take a look at socialization to help bring the vagus nerve back to a sense of normalcy, and finally, we will take a look at meditation.

Methods in Fighting off Depression

Probiotics to Stimulate the Vagus Nerve

Every digestive system is jam-packed with bacteria. It lines most of your digestive tract, allowing your body to digest the food within your guts essentially. The type of bacteria that is good for you and you want to have in your guts are known as probiotics. These are found already in many naturally fermented foods or other foods that are cultured. Take a look at the yogurt label the next time you are at the store—you may see that it is labeled as having a live culture. That live culture is all of the bacteria that you can eat and then seed into your digestive system.

When you do this, you can essentially boost the power of your digestive system. Even better, however, is the fact the digestive system can realty influence your mind. Having the right gut biome is essential when it comes to being able to function accordingly. Wishing to be able to function, you must have the right kinds of bacteria to create the right kinds of hormones your body will need.

In particular, Lactobacillus Rhamnosus and Bifidobacterium Longum are both associated with being able to help with stress hormones. They aid in the uptake of serotonin, and they also create positive changes to the GABA, a very important neurotransmitter for general regulation. When you do not have enough GABA in your body, it may impact your mood.

While science is still attempting to determine the exact details, it is believed when you do not have enough GABA, and you could end up suffering from anxiety, mood disorders (including depression), epilepsy, and chronic pain. Because of this explanation, it is super essential for you to recognize that the gut bacteria do impact the mind, and you need to ensure you honor that.

By taking probiotics with both Lactobacillus Rhamnosus and Bifidobacterium Longum, you can ensure that your body is going to have more of those proper bacteria that it will need to not only regulate the mood but also help with the vagus nerve as well. There are studies conducted that have shown results that mice tend to show fewer symptoms of anxiety and depression when they are given these necessary probiotics, and it is believed this is due to the vagus nerve.

Socialization to Stimulate the Vagus Nerve

Once again, we come right back to the social nervous system, the proposed method through which the vagus nerve regulates how we socialize. It has been found that socialization is one of the greatest ways to reduce stress, and this makes sense. Think about it—we are social creatures. If you want to alleviate stress, you need to be around people you love and care about. This socialization can leave you feeling fulfilled and better than ever.

In particular, many therapies also entertain the idea that to treat depression, you must be willing to go out on a limb and force the point. Many of them say the only way to get moving again with your anxiety or depression is to make sure you go out. You have to sort of reboot the mind into seeing it as enjoyable and beneficial—sound familiar?

When you suffer from depression, you frequently do not want to do anything at all, and yet, going out there and actively beginning to stimulate your vagus nerve through being out and exposed to other people is one of the most effective manners that you can use. It is essential for you to familiarize the ways you can spend that time with people and how getting out there can slowly, but surely begin to engage your vagus nerve.

This does not mean you have to go out to a party tonight; instead, take it slowly. Allow yourself too, little by little, is to better cope with the way that you are behaving. Over time, you will find you are better able to focus. Over time, you will find that this time you spend out and about is worth it. You will feel like you can, and you will be able to do everything you need to do.

Get up and get out. Get moving. Be social. Even if you just spend a few minutes with someone every day, having a conversation with them at the coffee shop as you wait for your order, you are still engaging with other people. As they engage with you, you will find that, little by little; you will be able to get back to functioning and be able to feel the whole within your own body again.

Meditation to Stimulate the Vagus Nerve

Finally, the last method we are going to consider in terms of what you can do with yourself to stimulate the vagus nerve for depression is to take a look at how you can meditate. Meditation is an incredibly powerful state of mind, and it has been found to activate those same areas within the brain that are triggered by the vagus nerve as well, implying that the two are related.

When you meditate, you are entering a quiet, stable state in which you can relax and focus on how you are feeling. You focus on the clarity and the peace within yourself and in doing so, you can slowly but surely seek solace within yourself.

Meditation is something people sometimes resist, but the truth of the matter is it is surprisingly powerful. You do not have to go out and suddenly let go of anything you enjoy to get out there and meditate. On the contrary, you can usually do it anywhere for any amount of time with very little commitment required. All you will need is yourself and a quiet place to rest, uninterrupted and left alone to enjoy the peace within yourself.

- Begin by finding a nice, quiet place for yourself where you can relax without intervention. Make sure that it is somewhere you will be able to better focus without any distractions.

- Take a deep breath in and hold it. Then, breathe out. Repeat this process, getting used to the way your breath feels.

- Find a position that you are comfortable sitting within. It could be any position at all; it does not have to be any particular one. All that matters is you are comfortable in it.

- Slowly shift your focus to your breathing. Let yourself continue to focus on just your breathing at this point, paying attention to the air coming in and out of your lungs.

- Any time that you feel your attention leave your breathing, you must quietly and gently shift it back, free from any judgment and free from any concern.

- Stay in this phase for as long as you feel comfortable, preferably at least five minutes.

Chapter 7. Vagus Nerve Relation to Anxiety

There are no other reasons for the truth that the vagus nerve can be used to deal with many health conditions. Anxiety is one of the conditions that can be completely managed through the stimulation of the vagus nerve.

What is Anxiety?

Anxiety is a natural state of the body in which a person experiences emotion, characterized by feelings of tension, worry, and physical changes such as blood pressure. Psychologists do not classify anxiety as a mental disorder. In normal life, every person has to deal with anxious moments from time to time. This state of emotion is what we refer to as anxiety. When a person is going through an anxious moment, they are generally worried and tense. Such a person experiences fear and nervousness. It is common for people to go through anxious moments, especially when facing a test or going through a tough emotional moment. If a person feels threatened, he/ she is likely to suffer a moment of anxiety.

However, when anxiety occurs persistently to a person, it can be classified as an anxiety disorder. The condition of anxiety disorder is the one treated as a medical condition and needs to be catered for. An anxiety disorder is a serious mental condition that should be diagnosed and treated as soon as possible. Here, we will be looking at the use of the vagus nerve to treat anxiety disorders. However, before we come to the treatment part, we must first understand the differences between anxiety and anxiety disorders. For many people, it is not easy to diagnose or spot the symptoms of an anxiety disorder. This is mainly because the symptoms are similar to the ones shown by a person during anxiety.

It often takes the intervention of a professional psychologist to diagnose anxiety disorders. In essence, the main difference between anxiety and anxiety disorders is the severity and duration. The recurrence of the anxious moment and the time it takes to fade away can be used to differentiate the disorder from any other passing moment of anxiety. The severity of an anxious moment is, in most times, proportional to the trigger. This is to mean that anxiety is a triggered moment of nervousness. Many factors contribute to anxiety, but one of the most relevant causes is an emotional association with past life experiences. People who have suffered any emotional pain in the past are likely to be triggered into anxiety by any item or person that reminds them of past experiences. In other words, a person who has suffered pain will experience fear or tension when they come in contact with the cause of the pain. For instance, if you have lost your leg in a car accident, you may feel anxious when traveling in a car. The thought of the traumatic accident makes the person feel anxious when traveling in a car. This person associates traveling in a car with horrible accidents.

When a person suffers from anxiety disorders, there is a development of physical signs such as nausea and high blood pressure. These only occur due to the physiological changes that trigger the occurrence of emotions. Before an emotion can occur in a person, the body undergoes various physiological changes. For instance, when a person experiences fear, there is coordination between the brain and the nervous system that leads endocrine glands to secrete some hormones. In the case of fear, the adrenal gland produces adrenaline, which in turn facilitates other chemical reactions. This explains why you may spot a person sweating or heavy breathing when they are afraid. When the fight or flight state of the body gets into the action, several hormones work to generate natural activities in the body that prepare a person for confrontation. Anxiety is one of those moments when a person is in a state of fight or flight. Unfortunately, anxiety, unlike fear, lasts for longer periods. The tension may last for hours or even days. If a person is in a constant state of anxiety, they may continuously affect the blood pressure and normal physiological process. For this reason, any person who suffers from anxiety must get assistance in dealing with the condition.

Anxiety is also related to having recurrent intrusive thoughts of negativity and concerns. When a person continuously experiences negativity, he/she may develop concerns towards such thoughts. These concerns and constant worry are what we refer to as anxiety. When a person is anxious, it is easy for them to get drawn into a daily routine of worry. This type of continuous action of worry is what develops into anxiety disorders.

Signs of Anxiety

Treating anxiety disorders come after diagnosis. In other words, before you think about undergoing treatment for anxiety, you should first get diagnosed. No person can get diagnosed without the ability to read signs. You can only offer help to close family members if you know how to read the signs and symptoms. As already mentioned, some of the symptoms of anxiety disorders may appear during normal anxious moments. Observing only a few signs does not mean that a person suffers from anxiety disorders. If a person suffers from anxiety, you will be able to observe multiple of the following signs occurring recurrently.

Restlessness: Any person suffering from anxiety is likely to experience impatience and restlessness. The tension caused by a continuous flow of negative thoughts may make a person feel edgy.

Uncontrollable Feelings of Worry: The other way to determine whether a person is suffering from anxiety or not is by listening to them. If a person is anxious, he/she is constantly worried about the future.

Increased Irritability: Irritability is a situation where a person easily gets angered. When a person is anxious, he/she is likely to get angry even without doing anything provocative.

Concentration Difficulties: Another serious sign of anxiety is a lack of concentration. A person who is suffering from anxiety is likely to undergo continuous thoughts of negativity.

Sleep Difficulties: Insomnia is one of the conditions associated with overthinking. Any person suffering from anxiety is likely to experience problems such as oversleeping or failing to sleep.

All the above signals are a normal part of life. If you are experiencing a tough and emotional moment, for example, during the loss of a job or loss of a loved one, you may experience some, if not all, of the above signs. However, the case where a person is classified as suffering from anxiety disorders involves a person who receives these signs continuously. If you continue experiencing signs of anxiety for days or weeks, you need to start looking for solutions. Anxiety disorders come in episodes that last for a few days to weeks. Some disorders only last a few hours. To better understand the occurrence and symptoms of anxiety disorders, let's have a look over the available types of anxiety disorders.

- Generalized Anxiety Disorder
- Panic Attacks
- Specific Phobia
- Agoraphobia
- Selective Mutism
- Social Anxiety Disorder or Social Phobia
- Separation Anxiety Disorder

How to Deal with the Anxiety Vagus Nerve

We have already recognized the truth that the nervous system is divided into parasympathetic and sympathetic functions. These two functions contract each other. To understand the relationship between the vagus nerve and anxiety, we must first understand the actions taken by the two aspects of the nervous system. In simple terms, the sympathetic nervous system is used to prepare the body for action. The production of hormones, such as adrenaline, only helps to prepare the body for action. On the other hand, the parasympathetic section of the nervous system only helps the body to get into a state of rest.

The anxiety only starts when a person experiments a stressful situation. When you are exposed to a stressful situation, the sympathetic nervous system is automatically activated. If the stress continues and it takes too long for the body to shut down the activated physiological changes, the body will suffer a lot of problems. For instance, when the sympathetic system starts to work, a person cannot experience parasympathetic actions such as sleep. We all know that rest is important for the body, and without rest, you are likely to suffer.

At the brain level, if the stress continues for long, two pathways are simultaneously activated (hypothalamus-pituitary-adrenal axis and the brain-intestine axis). Normally, the brain responds to stress (anxiety) by producing more hormones CRFs. The hormones travel from the hypothalamus to the pituitary glands, where they activate the production of other hormones known as (ACTH). Once ACTH is produced, it travels to the adrenal glands through the bloodstream, to activate cortisol and adrenal induction. When the adrenal glands are activated, they act as the immune system to prevent any internal injuries due to the stress. If the stress is continuing or chronic, the physiological changes in the body are likely to overwhelm the ability of the body to handle and function. Ultimately, the combination of the stress and the failure of the body may lead to devastating effects such as depression. Depression has been linked with inflammatory brain responses in many studies. Given that stress itself is an inflammatory precursor, it is essential to find a way of dealing with the stress before it extends to unmanageable levels.

Chronic stress can also lead to excessive production of glutamate. This neurotransmitter is known to cause migraines when produced in excess. Some research findings have also linked depression and anxiety to excessive production of glutamate. The stress on a person can lead to other mental problems too. For instance, the increased production of cortisol can reduce the volume of the hippocampus, the part of the brain responsible for the formation of new memories. This explains why people who suffer from anxiety easily forget new information.

The involvement of the vagus nerve in dealing with stress may lead to complications. Since the vagus nerve is unable to activate the relaxation signals, the sympathetic nervous system stays in control, leading to insomnia, gastrointestinal problems, and difficulty in breathing, among others.

According to research done by Miami University, the state of anxiety of a mother can affect the unborn baby too. It was found that women who suffer from depression or experience much anger during pregnancy had a similar vagal activity with their newborn babies. When a person is suffering from anxiety, vagal activity is reduced, since the vagus nerve only focuses on the sympathetic functions. To increase the vagal activity and reduce the anxiety, you must stimulate your vagus nerve.

We have already mentioned that there are varied ways of stimulating the vagus nerve. As we delve deeper, we will have a look at some of the healthy ways of stimulating your nerve for depression and anxiety.

Chapter 8. The Relation between The Vagus Nerve and Phobia & Trauma

The Vagus Nerve and the Phobias

People often hear about or experience others having a fear of certain things, and that's not necessarily worrisome. Still, when it grows fiercer and intense, it's something to be worried about. The fear from a sure thing, situation, or an entity when grows more potent, it is termed as a phobia. Phobias are of so many types, and they are all intense whatever kind they are. Also, it's impossible to escape it because it's an unavoidable fact of human life. Hey! Don't bite your nails out of fear now! The vagus nerve has the solution to your problem, but before jumping in, let's find out the biological presence of phobia in a human brain and its types (of course, not all!).

Phobia, unlike fear, is not a rush of terror that just passes away when the horror movie ends. These are mental disorders that even doctors diagnose in patients. The patients, when coming in contact with what triggers their phobia either freeze, get a panic attack, forget to breathe, and face intense distress and in some cases, they die too out of a heart attack. Yes, it's that serious! Now, what causes phobia?

It often starts in childhood; it could be acquired from a parent or a family member. Also, some events cause this, such as a near-death experience involving an object or an entity which then begins to haunt them for a lifetime. It could be a drowning experience where they got lucky and saved in time, and it could be a terrifying or a traumatic event involving darkness. It could be anything, and there are no specific causes. Now, when the brain witnesses all of that, it stores it somewhere and then replay it in the mind after being triggered to do so; that is when the object, situation, or entity they are afraid of appears in front of them. These chemical reactions take place in the amygdala, which causes the stress to overpower the patient, and they feel great fear surfacing, namely their phobia. Now, let's discuss its symptoms which are:

- The person who has a phobia would experience anxiety when exposed to the object which they fear.
- They would avoid that sure thing at all cost.
- They cease to function well when they come face to face with that thing they fear.
- The patients will also acknowledge how irrational their fear is and how they don't have anything to do with it.

Also, the physical effects bombard the patient, which are:

- Dizziness
- Sweating
- Dry mouth
- Pins and needles
- Butterfly in the stomach
- Headache
- Nausea
- Accelerated heartbeat
- Confusion and alienation
- A choking sensation
- Shivering
- Chills
- Hot flushes
- Abnormal breathing

These are the symptoms; also, there are signs such as people becoming clingy.

When you notice such things in yourself or the people around you, worry not! It can be efficiently dealt with.

There are many types of phobias, some of them are:

1. Glossophobia: Fear of public speaking.
2. Claustrophobia: Fear of small places.
3. Aquaphobia: Fear of water.
4. BII (Blood, injury and injection) phobia: The name says it all.
5. Tunnel phobia: Fear of tunnels.
6. Nyctophobia: Fear of the dark.
7. Acrophobia: Fear of heights.
8. Zoophobia: Fear of animals.
9. Astraphobia: Fear of thunder and lighting.
10. Aerophobia: Fear of flying.
11. Arachnophobia: Fear of spiders.
12. Haphephobia: Fear of touching or being touched.
13. Amaxophobia: Fear of driving a car.
14. Amaxophobia: Fear of untidiness.
15. Atychiophobia: Fear of failure.

All these fears have a history etched to them; for instance, people afraid of Haphephobia may have a history of sexual assault. Similarly, people having Acrophobia may have a near-death experience involving falling from any height. Just like that, there are specific reasons people develop these phobias, and they grow gradually as people grow. But be delighted! Vagus nerve is there to put an end to your fears and phobias and let you live a quality life. How?

Well, let's check it out!

Our vagus nerve is joined to our brain from one end and the other to all the organs of the body, it is the one that commands the brain to execute orders, therefore, when the panic rise and the phobia is triggered, the vagus nerve is stimulated and causes the fight or flight response to emerging. This helps the person get out of the situation quicker by fighting it or flying it. The therapists make use of specific techniques that stimulate the vagus nerve of the people. They let the patients face, deliberately, what they fear and have a phobia of. With this exposure, they instruct the patient to take deep breaths which are the vagus nerve stimulators. The therapists also ask the patient to sit back and relax, which also, is a vagus nerve stimulator.

So, when the fear begins to wash over the patient, the vagus nerve stimulation process and steps are applied to them, and the doctors even ask them to exercise and consult a friend to let it all loose. This ultimately causes them to relax and strengthen themselves against their phobias.

Told you! It's a lifesaver!

The Vagus Nerve and Trauma

Trauma is an emotional as well as a psychological response to any frightening and a shockingly heart-wrenching event. These events range from accidents to natural disasters, and calamities human mind takes time to get over or goes in deep shock after witnessing them. These incidents cause people to be overcome by shock, and at times, it causes them to go into denial. This often results in profuse sadness after the damaging event such as the death of a beloved, a severe injury, a breakup, verbal humiliation, or insult at some point in life or any other painful happenings. Trauma depends on the human brain and its capacity to remember every single detail about the happiness absorbing event that occurred to cause them sleepless nights and panic attacks.

Now, there are three types of traumas that are very common in people, and these are the ones that cause distress to strengthen its roots in the hearts of people, let's find out the names of the culprits:

Complex trauma:

It is a recurring trauma, and this occurs in a particular environment and situation. This causes the person to have panic attacks when exposed to a particular object or thing. It keeps growing intense if not treated on time.

Post-traumatic stress disorder (PTSD):

Many individuals are aware of this trauma that is very popular amongst people of different ages, and this occurs after a bone-chilling, heartbreaking event. It could be any experience associated with physical harm or any near-death experience. People who have PTSD are often hit with chilling thoughts, flashbacks, and memories of the event that caused the trauma to remain etched to them.

Developmental trauma disorder:

This disorder refers to the one where the person, mainly a child of age below 4, have trouble getting attached to any adult who tries to be caregivers. This usually occurs after mental or physical abuse or when the child is ignored or abandoned. It affects the mind of a little kid and makes them traumatic. Sad but true.

The person gets hit with unpredictable emotions, and they are bombarded with flashbacks that refresh in their minds the memories of that trauma. People fail to manage their emotions that come from every nook and corner, uninformed. This puts stress on the human mind and often causes strained relationships, questionable behavior, gloomy mood, lack of interest in life, and at times paranoia. This is what trauma seems like and how it affects people. Let's talk about its symptoms to identify it abruptly; hence, to treat is quickly by activating your vagus nerve. The signs and symptoms are:

The physical symptoms:

- Headache
- Nausea

The other symptoms:

- The constant guilt
- Shame or fear
- Flashbacks
- Clandestine emergence of different emotions
- Intense feeling of loneliness
- Anger
- Hopelessness
- Sadness and despair
- Shock
- Denial
- Feeling of alienation
- Self-blame
- Insomnia
- Nightmares
- Fatigue
- Getting startled easily

- Aches and pain
- Muscle tension

And a lot more, this is the reason many wellness-experts call trauma a lousy reaction of events that abundantly affect the mental health of a person and let them part ways with peace. The dominant method which helped the trauma patients is the stimulation of the vagus nerve. A very famous doctor, Doctor Scaer mentions in his book named, 'The Body Bears the Burden' that the traumatic memories are stored in a particular part of the brain that regulates the body. Therefore, traumatic stress often occurs when any trigger causes the memory to play before them. Now, let's see how the vagus nerve helps get rid of the traumatic stress and helps the person to overcome the trauma:

The vagus nerve deals with human emotions to a great extent, and when the long-term trauma strikes a person, just like anxiety and depression, it alleviates the trauma too, in no time. According to some experts, it is that magic fix required to eradicate any mental issue because big or small, it causes unrest to birth in mind and affects the entire system. Also, the brain does not function well when the unrest has strengthened its root in it. But everything is possible if you believe. Similarly, the vagus nerve combats and trounces the trauma. All we need to do to finish is to stimulate it through many stimuli. Such as:

- Coldwater –splashing cold water on the face or have a cold shower.

- Take care of your gut (mentioned for the zillionth time, I know.)

- Laugh aloud and a lot, you need endorphins, a lot of them.

- Breathe, take deep, belly breaths; the most popular way to activate the vagus nerve.

- Dance more! Yes! Shake a little and release it all. Have you ever seen any animal shaking from head to toe in a specific pattern? That's because it keeps them happy and stress-free. The best way to deal with trauma, isn't it?

- Exercise for maintaining the vagal tone.

- Do what makes you happy. This also keeps you away from having traumatic stress.

Chapter 9. The Vagus Nerve and Anger

One final area that the vagus nerve addressed that we are going to consider is the vagus nerve and anger. Anger is an incredibly powerful emotion. It is necessary to keep you alive in the wild. It encourages you to fight to protect yourself from a threat and to ensure that anyone around you is willing and able to respect your boundaries. When you suffer from problems with your vagus nerve, however, you may find that you have some issues regulating your mood, especially your anger.

Anger

Anger is usually categorized as an emotion in which you feel antagonistically toward someone else that has wronged you. It is a good thing in some ways—it encourages you to protect yourself and to express your frustration if things are not going as planned or expected. However, it can also be a big problem for people to face if they find that they are angry much of the time. Being angry too often can have significant health problems for you. It can lead you to having higher blood pressure. It can lead to you struggling to make friends with other people. It can fracture and even destroy friendships and relationships sometimes. Anger is powerful and essential, but in many ways, it is also quite dangerous.

Anger itself is one of your core emotions. It is the fight response when you go into sympathetic activation. This means that, often, it is a secondary emotion. It is usually in response to some threat that needs to keep handled effectively. It ties to feelings such as needing to protect yourself or those around you. It is necessary to keep you alive, and for that reason, it should be respected.

However, if you are not in a life-or-death situation, it can often go overboard. You can get far angrier than you have intended to. It can cause you to make poor decisions that are not particularly effective in that particular situation. It can result in you doing things that you usually would not, all because you are stressed out and angry.

The activation of anger is associated with all sorts of stress hormones. These stress hormones tend to impair your ability to think correctly while also causing problems with the immune system. The bottom line is that your anger is a necessary part of you, but it is something that needs to be controlled, so it does not get out of hand. You are playing with fire when you are angry, and it takes plenty of time and focus on ensuring that you are not getting burnt when you are.

When Anger Becomes a Problem

Of course, everyone experiences anger to some degree. It is a standard part of being human, and there is no real way to get around it. However, it will reach a part where it is a problem and impacting, not only your current situation, but your entire life and the lives of those around you. In particular, anger begins to become problematic when you can identify that it is directly causing other problems for you. It may interfere with your relationships, causing you to struggle to make sure that you can ever solve any conflicts that you have. It can interfere with your ability to perform effectively at work, leading to you potentially losing your job. It can be related to you committing a crime when caught up in your anger—if you were to hurt someone else in your anger, for example, you would likely end up facing legal repercussions.

There is no clear-cut line where anger moves from a normal human emotion into a problem. You must be able to decide that for yourself—if you think that your anger is a problem, then it probably is. If you think that your anger is directly related to you having issues in life, then it may be a problem that you have to address.

Anger and the Vagus Nerve

Remember, anger is the fight in the fight or flight response. It is designed to fight off your enemies or fend off threats. However, when you struggle with doing so, you are going to find that you are stuck in your anger. Of course, you can begin to regulate your anger through the use of your parasympathetic nervous system.

Just as with the vast majority of the other conditions that is within this book so far, being able to activate your parasympathetic response will help you eliminate the anger. Your parasympathetic nervous system acts as an emotional regulator. It is what allows you to make sure that you are going to be able to pull yourself away from emotions and re-center yourself. It allows you to calm yourself down. It allows yourself to begin to think clearly because your body is preparing to rest, which will then allow it to focus on digesting.

You may already use methods related to vagus nerve activation when you are trying to calm down from an anger episode. In particular, people tend to make use of breathing deeply. This triggers the vagus nerve almost instantly, leading to a drop in blood pressure and, usually, a reduction in anger as well thanks to that trigger. When you take your deep breaths, you usually find that the body responds by immediately calming down and leaving you feeling more prepared to tackle the world around you.

Chapter 10. How to Activate the Vagus Nerve

There is one method of Vagus nerve healing that does require surgery. Called Vagus Nerve Stimulation (VNS), this surgery started in the 90s as a treatment for epilepsy. This surgery is part of the emerging field of bioelectronics medicine. VNS surgery nowadays embeds a tiny electronic device, similar to a pacemaker, into the chest. A thin wire, called a lead, runs from the device to the central trunk of the Vagus nerve in the spinal cord. Once implanted, this device sends tiny electrical pulses to the Vagus nerve at regular intervals to keep it stimulated and fully functional. This is quite an invasive procedure, and so comes with all of the risks that accompany any surgery. Some notable side effects documented with this procedure are sore throat and difficulty swallowing. Some people have also experienced changes in voice, shortness of breath, coughing, slow heart rate, stomach discomfort, and nausea (Carter, 2019). However, despite these side effects, this procedure has passed a number of clinical trials as a treatment for both epilepsy and rheumatoid arthritis (Carter, 2019). Knowing what we know about the Vagus nerve, one can safely assume that this procedure would be sufficient for a number of different health problems.

Using a Vagus nerve stimulating device is not the only way to activate the benefits associated with the Vagus nerve. There are many things that you can do from the comfort of your own home that make it just as simple to activate your Vagus nerve. These things done at home will be more for your overall well-being and less for your severe cases and chronic illnesses, but you can still benefit just as much. Here are a few of our favorite techniques used to keep everything in check.

Alternatively, there are a number of home-based methods that are also used to stimulate this nerve. When a device becomes needed, it is usually in order to treat cases of epilepsy and depression that haven't been able to respond to other medical treatments such as pharmaceuticals or psychotherapy.

The device is located under the skin of the chest or neck, with a wire connecting it to the Vagus nerve itself. The device can then send signals through the Vagus nerve to your brain stem where it can then process the information given to your brain. The device would typically be programmed and controlled by a trained neurologist, but the patient will often receive a handheld magnet too, that can also help them to control their own device. There are studies currently conducted with the hopes that in the future, the stimulation of the Vagus nerve can also have applications to treat other conditions such as Alzheimer's disease, migraines and cluster headaches, as well as multiple sclerosis.

By stimulating the Vagus nerve, we have found that we can improve on certain conditions such as the following:

- Heart disease, which is a condition involving blood clots to the heart as well as diseased blood vessels and structural problems with the heart itself.
- Tinnitus, which causes a buzzing or ringing sound in your ears that you may associate with hearing loss. This ringing noise may be a constant sound, or it may come and go.
- Obesity, which is a condition of a person's weight, whereby they fall on the larger end of the scale and can develop other secondary issues on top of their weight.
- Alcohol addiction where a person ultimately becomes utterly dependent on alcohol in order to function in society.
- Migraines are painful headaches, often causing a loss of balance, eye sensitivity to light, as well as seeing 'spots' or patterns in vision.
- Anxiety disorders whereby a person may experience substantial and uncontrollable feelings of worry, stress, or fear to the point that it interferes with the person's daily routine in society and leaves them unable to function correctly.
- Alzheimer's disease, which is a progressive disease that takes over a person's mental functions and destroys their memory.
- Leaky gut syndrome, which is a gastrointestinal digestive condition where toxins and bacteria are able

to 'leak' through the intestinal wall, affecting the rest of the body.
- Inadequate blood circulation, which is often caused by a buildup of plaque within the arteries and blood vessels resulting in stiffness in your limbs as well as severe pain.
- Mood disorders, which are classified generally as extreme highs or extreme lows. This is an elevation or lowering of someone's mood for a short period of time.
- Cancer, whereby abnormal cells within the body will uncontrollably divide themselves and destroy body tissue and healthy cells along the way.

With Vagus nerve stimulation, we can say that approximately 80% of its nerve fibers are meant to send information from the body and organs to the brain, while the other 20% of nerve fibers will send information back from the brain to the rest of the body.

Before we dive into the types of VNS, AANS has specific guidelines with regards to whom this is suited for. People unsuitable for this treatment will have one of the following conditions:

- Undergoing some other form of brain stimulation
- Heart issues or abnormalities
- Lung diseases

- Vasovagal syncope (a condition where a person faints due to a sudden drop in blood pressure)
- Abnormalities in the central nervous system
- Gastric ulcers
- Existing throat issues or hoarseness

There are two types of VNS methods that doctors apply. Generally speaking, they're administered to patients who suffer from treatment resistant depression or epilepsy. By "treatment resistant" I mean that depression symptoms exist despite repeated medication and other treatment options applied. In other words, VNS is a last resort and even then, it is used in conjunction with other methods to deliver relief.

Take Care of Your Digestive Tract

All of the health of all your digestive tract is incredibly important for your body to function and it also plays an essential role in the functioning of your Vagus nerve. Your gut is made up of the theocentric nervous system that is a 'microbiome' surviving inside your digestive system.

This little ecosystem contains hundreds and thousands of good bacteria that hold the balance in your digestive system and keep your body healthy and functioning. This good bacterium that lives inside your intestinal tracts allows the body to help move digested food through your stomach.

If there is an imbalance in this good bacteria, or if an illness takes over, your digestive system sounds its own alarm of sorts and triggers an inflammatory response within your immune system and therefore causes a wide range of disruptive responses to your body, such as nausea and vomiting as well as anxiety and depression.

Shake it off

We are quite confident that Taylor Swift was onto something here when she sang "Shake it off." These words, when associated with the Vagus nerve, are inspired by how animals would have a good shake off in the wild in order to release physical tension or to come out of a freeze response after being in complete panic mode.

You can use shaking as a simple practice to release your tension, too! Firstly, think about where you are tense as well as what has made you tense. Feel through your body to create self-awareness of what is happening around you as well as within you.

Feels good, doesn't it?

It's getting a Bit Chilly Here

So, it turns out that exposure to cold temperatures can also give the Vagus nerve a bit of a jolt.

This is because exposing the Vagus nerve to a sudden drop in temperatures stimulates the cholinergic neurons that cross at specific points. By stimulating these receptors, you are forcing the body to go into a fight or flight shock that jolts you into the sympathetic nervous system. From there, the body is able to calm down using the parasympathetic nervous system, giving both sides of this nerve a good bit of exercise along the way.

Alternatively, if you live in a toasty warm climate and have sweat dripping off of the end of your nose on a daily basis, you may find this practice to be quite pleasant and refreshing! Whichever way it works for you in the long run, as long as your heart rate kicks it up a notch, it's useful.

You can reduce stress or anxiety by reducing the sympathetic nervous response to stressors. Cold exposure can boost parasympathetic activity, which helps bring down the fight and flight response. It can also help reduce stomach issues. If you feel sick, being exposed to cold can often reverse the feeling of nausea that you feel.

Studies have shown that cold on the neck is the most effective, so try putting a cold washcloth on the back of your neck for best results.

Diaphragmatic Breathing

Most people will inhale up to 14 times per minute and in doing so, have shallow breathing. When you become more self-aware of your breathing rate, you are able to lower the amount to a more ideal breathing rate of 6 inhales per minute.

This forces your body to practice more profound breathing techniques and to fill your lungs to capacity with each breath. It's incredibly easy to practice this routine wherever you may be. I'm practicing it right now as I type! This type of breathing exercise especially helps to trigger the Vagus nerve and turns on full activation as it is telling the brain that it is now necessary to calm down, even though the nerve itself has not been given that particular instruction directly. In this way, the mechanism is the same as when you close your eyes and tap against your eyelids gently. Your brain will perceive each tap as a spark of light shining through.

When we breathe in deeper breaths, we are making use of the lower part of our chest and moving the diaphragm in such a way that it will promote relaxation.

Humming

Strange though it sounds, humming or singing stimulates the Vagus nerve because it's connected to the muscles of the throat. This knowledge lends a great deal of scientific credence to the healing power of chants, mantras, or syllables (such as the OM syllable) found in traditional religious or spiritual practices throughout the world. Sound healing, as well as listening to and playing music, have also been linked to the stimulation of the Vagus nerve. Many therapists have seen successful results treating conditions as varied as stuttering, depression, ADD, cognitive disorders, and hearing impairment with sound-based therapies.

Speaking. For the same reason, speaking can stimulate the Vagus nerve, but this must be low stress speaking. Positive social interactions, reading out loud to yourself, or reciting poetry are all speaking exercises that get the vocal cords vibrating in a way that stimulates the Vagus nerve.

Meditation. So many studies have been popping up recently about the positive health benefits of meditation, and stimulation of the Vagus nerve is definitely one of them.

The most vital thing to know and engrave in your mind is that healing doesn't happen overnight. Miraculous as the Vagus nerve's healing propensities are, you probably won't see results immediately. Remember always to be patient with your body, and to pay attention to the details. Small changes are often indicators of great work being done at the cellular level. If any healing strategies cause additional stress or pain to the body, don't continue them. There are so many ways to stimulate the Vagus nerve, you are guaranteed to find a healing practice that's right for you.

If your Vagus nerve isn't properly stimulated, it can lead to problems in your GI tract, so it's imperative to make sure it's working as best as it can.

Chapter 11. Methods to Activate the Vagus Nerve

Yoga

Yoga has been done and embraced for 5,000 years and more. What began as a spiritual and physical exercise in Northern India such a long time ago now practices across the entire world by people from a wide range of social backgrounds and pretty much every country on Earth.

There is a reason yoga is so popular: it works. Despite what some may believe, yoga is not just random practice. It's not mumbo-jumbo. And it's most definitely not a scam of any kind.

Multiple studies show that yoga is efficient in a multitude of ways. For starters, it is a very good physical exercise, no matter how you look at it. If you remove any spiritual meaning and any kind of mindfulness, yoga still involves some pretty good stretching. Many people believe that most of what Yoga proposes are impossible poses that cannot get performed unless you are already an expert. However, yoga can be adapted to all levels of fitness, and people can practice it with certain medical conditions as well (provided that, of course, they are monitored by a professional trainer specialized in helping these types of patients).

Yoga can be a real blessing for pretty much everyone who tries it - and there is plenty of research to back up this idea as well. Some of you might be familiar with the general benefits of yoga, but there is so much more to it!

Overall, any type of exercise can have almost the same effect on human health. Yoga is special, however, because it incorporates more than just physical exercise, bringing together three dimensions that are of the utmost importance in physical and mental health: The actual stretching (the physical exercise), meditation (mental exercise), and breathing.

All of these dimensions can be very directly correlated with activating the vagus nerve and allowing it to help people relax, manage their fears, and build a better social engagement system.

How is yoga connected to the vagus nerve? Because it engages the body in exercise and because it focuses a lot on breathing, Yoga can tap into the vagus nerve to activate it for a healthier and more balanced you, at a more general level and at the level of the specific medical conditions you may suffer from.

Meditation

Meditation is less of a physical exercise and more of a mental one. Yet, even though most meditation happens "in the head," it is important to mention here that there are many physical activities that incorporate meditation in them. Yoga is one of them, but you can say the same about tai-chi as well.

Meditation is good for you, and a long list of reasons. Even more, meditation has been proven to work in a variety of situations. Researchers studied its effects for decades now, and even researchers in some of the highest-regarded institutions of the world can attest to the integrity of its effectiveness.

It is important to mention that meditation alone can show mild improvement in one's anxiety, so further steps should be taken as well (Goyal, 2014). That does not translate, however, into any kind of proven inefficiency of meditation. Rather, it translates into an understanding that mental health takes a variety of approaches, and meditation can be one of the ingredients in the mix.

- It helps patients suffering from depression. Just as in the case of anxiety, meditation is helpful for patients suffering from depression. In a study conducted by Harvard, it was shown that depression could be ameliorated by the practice of meditation (Powell, 2018).

Also, as in the case of anxiety, simple meditation may not be enough (especially in more severe cases). However, meditation can provide patients with a good dose of help.

- It can change the way your brain functions, allowing it to manage stress, anxiety, and pain in a more successful way. Still, this benefit needed mentioning here, precisely because it lies at the foundation of many other positive changes that can occur in people's lives after picking up meditation.

- It has been shown to have positive effects on criminal rehabilitation, as well as helping patients recovering from substance abuse. It is not entirely clear why, but studies have also shown that meditation can prove efficient in helping former criminals and people who abused substances gain a more positive perspective on their lives and find their balance. The specific type of meditation presented in this study is transcendental meditation, but there is no evidence that other types of meditation might not have the same positive effect (Hawkins, 2003).

It is quite clear that meditation can alter not only how you think, but how you see yourself, your life, and others you meet along the way. It appears that meditation does have a pretty impactful effect on how the brain functions. More specifically, meditation can:

- Help in bias reduction.
- Increase focus.
- Be more positive.

Some findings show that meditation can also help your brain stay younger for a longer period (Luders, 2015). This could have implications on the aging of the entire body, as well as certain medical conditions that tend to be more common among seniors.

Meditation can also boost your cognitive abilities, especially learning and memory. In other words, it can make you smarter (Hölzel, 2011).

Emotion control can also be "taught" through meditation. Because this practice trains your brain to concentrate the thinking process on very specific areas and points of focus, it can also train it to have better control of emotions (including negative ones).

All in all, meditation can make borderline miracles when it comes to a wide range of benefits it can bring into someone's life. As you have read thus far, however, they are not just assumptions, but studied effects. We do not claim meditation is a cure-all (none of the therapies in this, and you should not believe anyone who says so). However, research shows that meditation can improve your life in numerous ways.

Foods

You might know that good nutrition is crucial for your health and your level of fitness. Nutrition is crucial from every point of view - and not just for your physical health, but your mental health as well.

We tend to be extremely connected with our food. We socialize over our holiday meals, we date, over dinner, and we tend to find refuge in comfort foods when things go bad as well. Even more, eating more or eating less than usual is considered to be one of the most common trigger sign of depression, showing that emotions and food have a very strong connection.

Nutrition is about a lot more than salads and macadamia nuts for a thin waistline and shiny hair. Living in the modern world, we tend to be easily swayed away from foods that provide us with fast comfort of being ultra-palatable, and we tend to forget that eating is not an act of war against our bodies, but an act of love.

Indeed, nutrition plays a massive role in how you feel and how you perceive life itself. Nobody says you cannot indulge in ice cream or that you cannot enjoy your Thanksgiving dinner with family. It's just that you have to know what true balance means.

It doesn't mean any kind of fad diet. No matter the need to promote extreme healthy diets, the truth is that no diet that restricts you from eating a certain group of foods can be truly balanced for you.

The good functioning of the vagus nerve is associated with everything you eat, so you should make sure that everything you put in your body is dense from a nutritional point of view and that it provides your real body value. Furthermore, some foods are considered to be more efficient in ensuring a healthy nervous system. Some of them include the following:

- Dark leaves (such as spinach and kale)
- Dark chocolate
- Broccoli
- Salmon and fatty fish
- Avocado

The beneficial effect of healthy fats on the vagus nerve has also been proven by research. According to a study done in 2005, good fats can inhibit inflammation in the body precisely because they tap into the vagus nerve. Although you could not necessarily call this "vagus nerve activation" in the full sense of the word, it is one of the easiest things you can do to improve the good functioning of this essential nerve in the human body (and the way it connects to other areas of the body as well) (Luyer, 2005).

Physical Therapy

Of all the therapies and treatments we are presenting, physical therapy is, by and large, one of the most highly regarded ones in terms of how often the medical community recommends it.

How is physical therapy related to the vagus nerve?

It might not always be. For example, for someone suffering from mental trauma, physical therapy might only bring the benefits any other type of exercise would. However, for someone who has suffered actual neurological damage in the vagus nerve region, physical therapy might be recommended.

It is worth noting that a lot of the neurological damage cannot be undone 100%. With physiotherapy, medication, and following the doctor's recommendations, however, patients can improve their state, and they can live a normal, healthy life in many situations.

You should practice physical therapy only with a professional, regardless of the recommendation you received to do it. Because it involves movement and technology that should be carefully monitored, there is no way you can become your own "physiotherapist." You absolutely shouldn't, because safety should be your primary concern from every point of view. The main reason we included it, here is that it is, without a doubt, one of the most successful treatments associated with the vagus nerve.

Breathing

This might be quite obvious, but this does not discuss simple breathing, but deep breathing. Incorporated in many other practices (including yoga, meditation, and physical therapy), deep breathing is one of the most recommended and efficient exercises for the vagus nerve.

Why does it work?

When you practice deep breathing, the neurons in your abdomen that are meant to detect high blood pressure will send a signal to your brain, and then to your vagus nerve, showing that the vagus nerve has to kick into action and lower the blood pressure. As a result, the entire vagus nerve will be activated, with all the benefits that come with this:

- Lower blood pressure
- Increased resistance to stress
- Management of anxiety and panic attacks
- Management of depression
- Healthier digestive system

You should practice deep breathing from the diaphragm. In other words, when you practice this exercise, you should inhale through your core, your abdomen, and see it fill in with air. When you exhale, your core will be emptied as well.

Conclusion

If I had told you at the start that there is one nerve in the body whose activity effectively controls our destinies, perhaps you wouldn't have believed me. It would still be hard to believe up until now, if not for the wealth of scientific resources one can find about this topic. There is a huge body of research on disparate topics, and all joined together only by the fact that the vagus nerve has something to do with them.

Perhaps it's a good time to appreciate the wonder and complexity of the human body. Many of us had been taught about the body as a sort of computer where the brain is the central processing unit, the heart is the battery, and the lungs and gut the power cords connecting us to the power supply that is food, water, and air. But the human body is instead an intricate and highly organic system, where even the mighty brain takes cues from the rest of the body. Every organ system has a hand in determining the next steps for the body, and somewhere in that great switchboard of information, the vagus nerve sits trying to sort everything out.

This book has taken you through the whole gamut of research and details on the vagus nerve. By now, you should know pretty much everything there is to know about it, from its anatomy to its myriad of functions, from harnessing it for overall health to the issues that it can address shortly.

But if there is one piece of info that you should never forget out of all that you have read, it is this: The vagus nerve is just a part of a network, a vast network of feedback and control, input and assessment that we have not yet completely explored and mapped. With all this information on the vagus nerve, it would be so easy to spend all your time trying to stimulate your vagus nerve to its optimal tone. Now, all that's good, but it's still just a part of the overall equation of health.

Remember that the vagus nerve does not just relay information from the brain to the rest of the body. It also actively picks up information from the rest of the body, sending it up to the brain. While one can (in the light of all the research we covered) assert that a person can only be as healthy as his vagus nerve, it would be more accurate to say that the vagus nerve could only be as healthy as the organ surrounding it.

You could have a perfectly functioning active vagus nerve, but you may still develop various illnesses thanks to your lifestyle choices. You may still be a victim of one of the GBDs. Note that while vagus stimulation can ward off certain issues, the vagus nerve is more or less just a mirror reflecting your state of overall health when it comes to other illnesses. It's so easy to confuse these two concepts. Stimulating your vagus nerve can't (at least not yet) cure cancer, but this cancer can show important signs when viewed through the vagus nerve.

In short, take care of the vagus nerve as much as you need — do the "bullet time" breathing exercises (or take a deep look at the contemplative traditions if you have time), fix your diet, do a routine vagal massage, and perk up your posture. When you feel that something is wrong with a different part of the body, seek ways to cure it independently of vagus stimulation — but let the stimulation continue as a means of augmenting whatever other remedies you may use.

Observing the vagus nerve up close shows us a very important lesson, too. We are exposed to the idea that what we know about the slew of diseases affecting the world might be the tip of the iceberg. With all the in-depth research we have, we just gradually become more and more aware of just how interconnected things are, and how seemingly disparate things can be deeply related because of an overarching factor. Who knew that reading in the EEG could predict whether or not you are likely to suffer from depression? Who knew that stimulating something other than the brain could help the brain repair itself from stroke? Who knew that the word "gut feel" actually has scientific backing, since the gut indeed talks to the brain? Who knew that the microbial flora in one's gut could even affect how moody a person can be?

One can only imagine the surprise of the first people who discovered the wonders of the vagus nerve. Today, that wonder lives on in the people who have had the opportunity to explore the powers of this twin bundle of nerve fibers winding its way through the human body. Just do a cursory search online, and you will be seeing a lot of articles hailing the vagus nerve as the body's best-kept secret to health, a holy grail of cures.

But again, be careful of such labeling. The vagus nerve isn't the Holy Grail — the human body, as a whole, is. We haven't even mapped the entirety of the vagus nerve yet, and science is still busy trying to find the best way to tame and stimulate it. But who knows if, in the future, we find some specific part of the vagus nerve — or a different part of the body, for that matter — that will concentrate all the nerve's powers into a smaller area? And then another one before that? The search for "the secret" will always continue, but never take your eyes off the fact that the body is a holistic system, meant to function as a whole.

Just like the meditation masters of old, may the knowledge you gained about the vagus nerve serve as building blocks on which you can build something synergistic — something that is at one with the body and everything that is around it.

Printed in France by Amazon
Brétigny-sur-Orge, FR